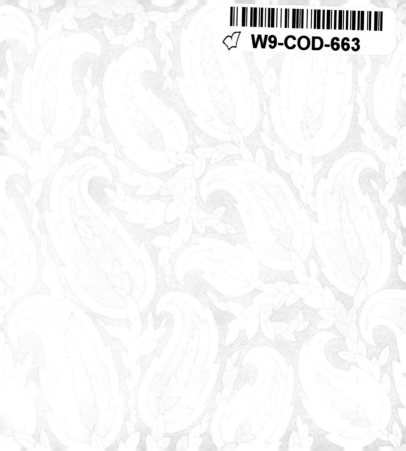

LITTLE WONDERS

THE WONDER OF

DAD

Phyllis Hobe

The C.R. Gibson Company
Norwalk, Connecticut 06856

LITTLE WONDERS

The Wonder of Mom
The Wonder of Dad
The Wonder of Friends
The Wonder of Babies
The Wonder of Little Girls
The Wonder of Little Boys

Published by The C.R. Gibson Company,
Norwalk, Connecticut 06856

Printed in the U.S.A.
Designed by Deborah Michel

ISBN 0-8378-7702-4
GB402

A dad can
make you believe
in yourself—
because he does.

A dad can persuade
you to do impossible
things like floating on
top of the water
after he lets go.

Dads help you
to make dreams
come true.

A dad starts planning your life the moment you're born—
by the time you're two, he starts revising it.

A dad is the only person you'll ever know who can put things together by reading the instructions.

A dad won't baby you when you get sick, but he'll lie awake all night just in case you need him.

A dad is always
a little sad when his
kids go off to play with
their friends because it's
the end of his second
childhood.

A dad can accept almost anything except the price of sneakers.

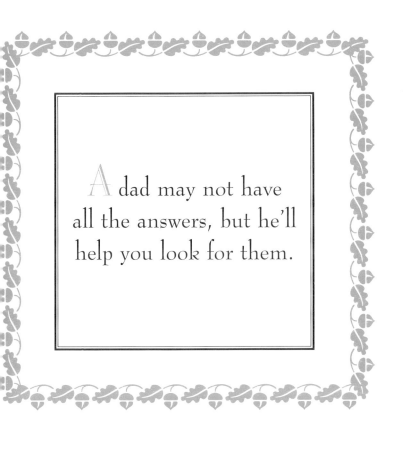

A dad may not have
all the answers, but he'll
help you look for them.

A dad may seem strict to you, but to your friends, he cares.

A dad gives you
the best seat in the
house by lifting you up
on his shoulders when
a parade goes by.

A dad has everything in his toolbox except whatever he needs to fix whatever is broken.

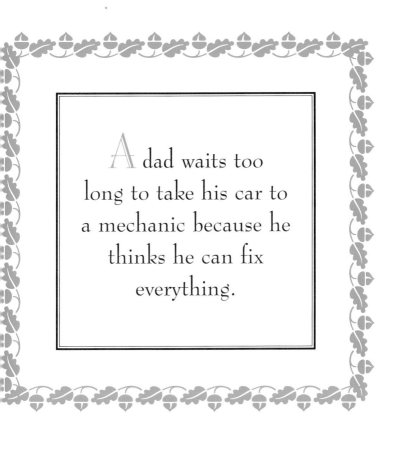

A dad waits too long to take his car to a mechanic because he thinks he can fix everything.

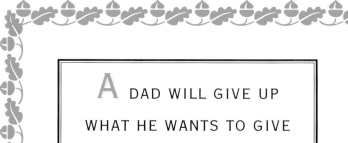

A DAD WILL GIVE UP
WHAT HE WANTS TO GIVE
YOU WHAT YOU NEED.

A DAD ENJOYS DOING
YOUR HOMEWORK,
EXCEPT NEW MATH.

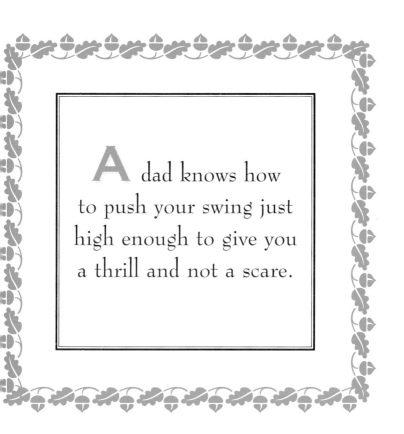

A dad knows how to push your swing just high enough to give you a thrill and not a scare.

A DAD IS GENEROUS

☞ *he'll let your snowman wear his favorite sweater...*

☞ *he'll buy that new cereal you want, and*

finish it if you don't like it...

❧

☞ *he'll stop whatever he's doing when you want to talk...*

❧

☞ *he'll let you learn to drive in his car.*

A dad will get
lost on a road that isn't
on his map because
his maps are older
than he is.

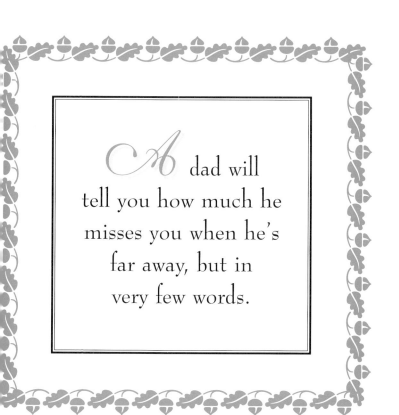

A dad will
tell you how much he
misses you when he's
far away, but in
very few words.

A dad sees the telephone as his enemy—it intrudes on his privacy, absconds with his family and threatens him with financial ruin.

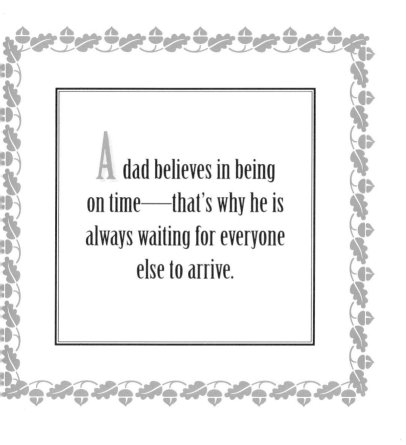

A dad believes in being on time—that's why he is always waiting for everyone else to arrive.

A dad forgives your mistakes but not his own.

A dad remembers walking to high school.

$\mathcal{A}$ dad will go anywhere he doesn't have to wear a tie.

A dad can turn a disappointment into a discovery—by opening your eyes to new directions... by telling you to try again—as many times as it takes.

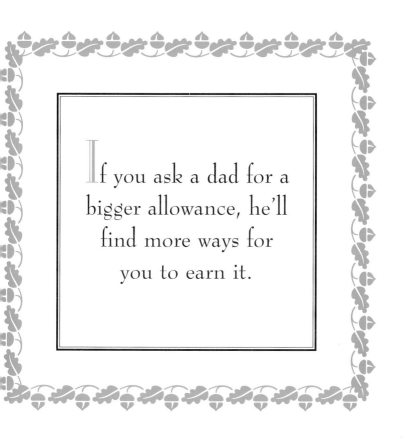

If you ask a dad for a bigger allowance, he'll find more ways for you to earn it.

A dad in the kitchen makes cooking a scientific expedition.

A dad may have grown up without knowing how to use a vacuum cleaner, but he's a fast learner.

A dad will always
take your advice.

A dad will say "Ask your
mother" when he doesn't
want to say "No."

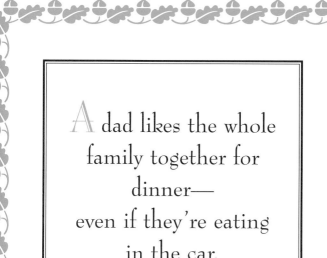

A dad likes the whole
family together for
dinner—
even if they're eating
in the car.

A dad lets you win a lot of games when you're little, but he doesn't want you to let him win when you're big.

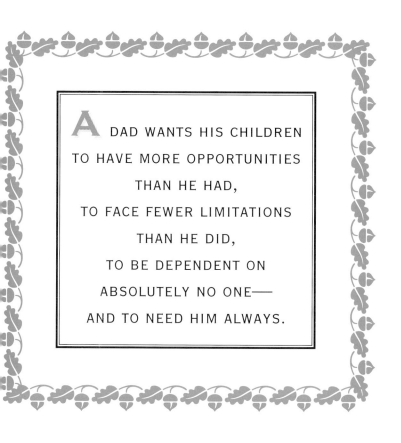

A DAD WANTS HIS CHILDREN
TO HAVE MORE OPPORTUNITIES
THAN HE HAD,
TO FACE FEWER LIMITATIONS
THAN HE DID,
TO BE DEPENDENT ON
ABSOLUTELY NO ONE—
AND TO NEED HIM ALWAYS.

A dad
tells you to
do the work
you like.

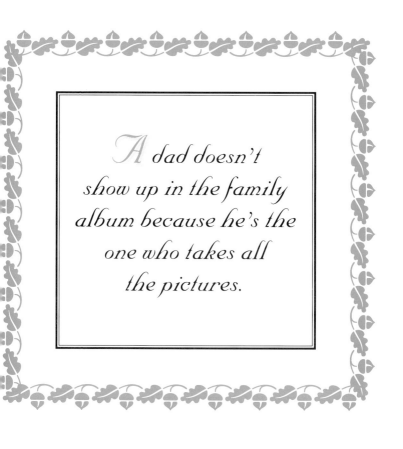

A dad doesn't show up in the family album because he's the one who takes all the pictures.

A dad can go
to a mall and buy
only what's on
his list.

A dad doesn't believe
that appliances can ever
wear out.

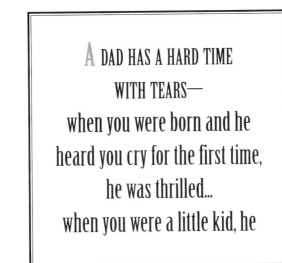

A DAD HAS A HARD TIME
WITH TEARS—
when you were born and he
heard you cry for the first time,
he was thrilled...
when you were a little kid, he

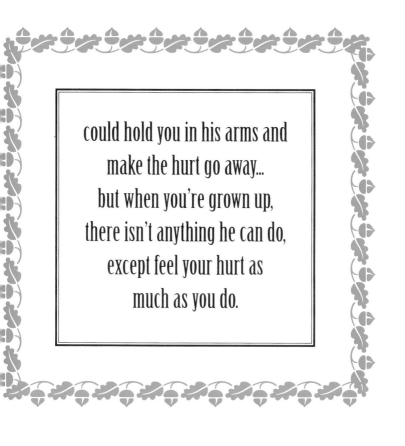

could hold you in his arms and
make the hurt go away...
but when you're grown up,
there isn't anything he can do,
except feel your hurt as
much as you do.

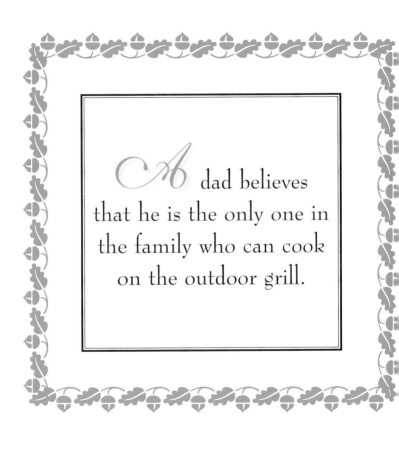

$\mathcal{A}$ dad believes that he is the only one in the family who can cook on the outdoor grill.

A dad will shake
your hand when you
leave home because if he
hugs you, he may not be
able to let go.

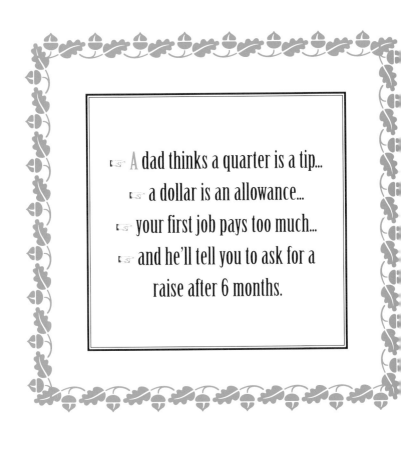

☞ A dad thinks a quarter is a tip...
☞ a dollar is an allowance...
☞ your first job pays too much...
☞ and he'll tell you to ask for a raise after 6 months.

A dad thinks people ought to stand on their own two feet, so—he won't tell you what to do but he'll let you know he doesn't agree.

A dad will keep a
promise to help a friend,
even if you ask him to
go fishing.

A dad will keep setting up the electric trains years after you lose interest in them because he still wants to play with them.

A dad wants your first car to be a tank... but when you get a sports car he'll want to test drive it— every Saturday.

A dad finds it hard to deal with thinning hair—so he blames his barber for taking too much off the top.

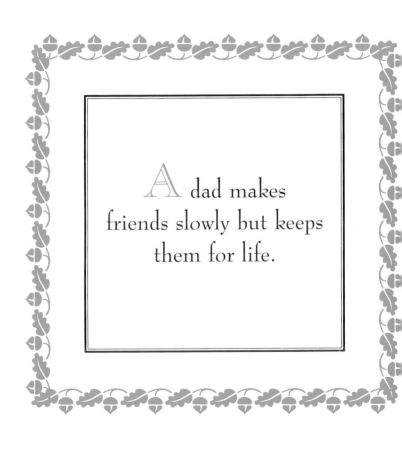

A dad makes friends slowly but keeps them for life.

A dad insists that your kids are much better behaved than you were.

A dad spends quality time with his kids.

A dad doesn't try to be the best... he just tries to do his best.

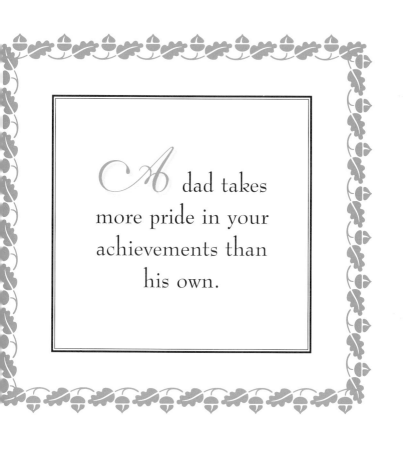

A dad takes more pride in your achievements than his own.

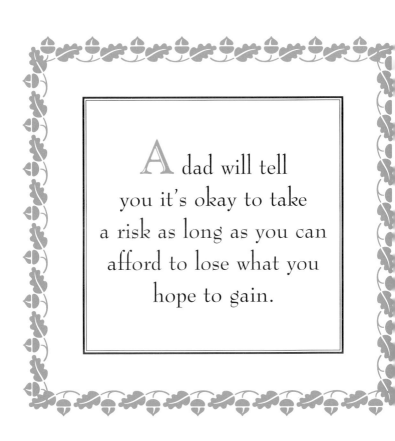

A dad will tell
you it's okay to take
a risk as long as you can
afford to lose what you
hope to gain.

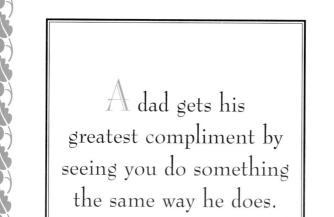

A dad gets his greatest compliment by seeing you do something the same way he does.

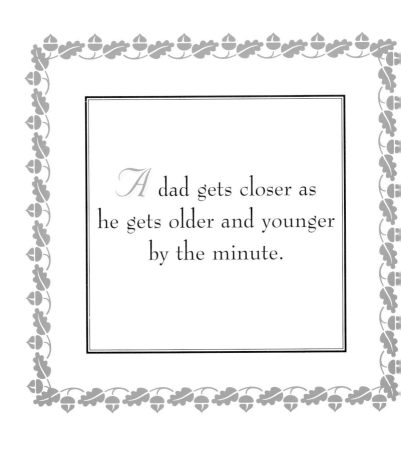

$\mathcal{A}$ dad gets closer as
he gets older and younger
by the minute.

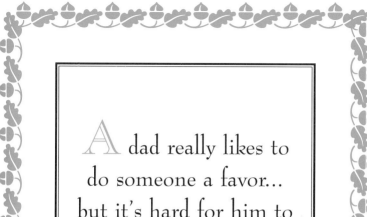

A dad really likes to
do someone a favor...
but it's hard for him to
ask for one.

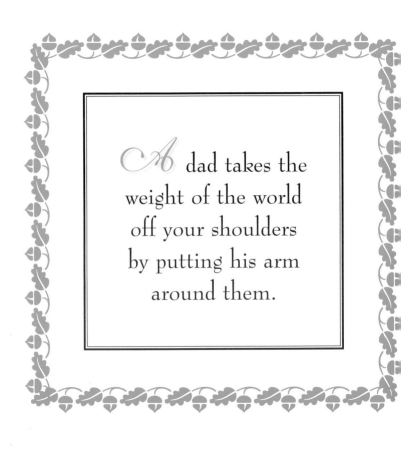

$\mathcal{A}$ dad takes the weight of the world off your shoulders by putting his arm around them.